Why We Are in Need of Tales

Why We Are in Need of Tales

discovering philosophical treasures in picture books

Maria daVenza Tillmanns

IGUANA

Publisher: Meghan Behse
Editor: Holly Warren
Front cover image: Lenard Guerrero
Back cover image: Laisha Delgado

All drawings used with the permission of the artists and their parent(s).

ISBN 978-77180-466-0 (hardcover)
ISBN 978-77180-465-3 (paperback)
ISBN 978-77180-467-7 (epub)

This is an original print edition of *Why We Are in Need of Tales*.

To all the young philosophers at El Toyon Elementary

Why We Are in Need of Sharing In

— *It's Mine* by Leo Lionni —

Huk and Tuk, the two characters in *Why We Are in Need of Tails* — remember those two? — decided to go to the middle of nowhere to have their cup of tea and tell each other tales.

They loved going to the middle of nowhere, because there is so much room for imagination.

Telling tales made them feel connected, sort of like when they felt connected when they had actual tails. But that was a long time ago, and that's another story.

It was a bright sunny day, and Huk and Tuk decided to sit down by a pond called Rainbow Pond, which was named after the pond in a famous tale by Leo Lionni — the greatest of tale-tellers.

You know, said Huk, there's an interesting story about this pond. Do you know the story?

No, said Tuk.

Well, Huk began, a long time ago, three quarrelsome frogs — Milton, Rupert and Lydia — lived on an island in this pond.

They fought all day long.

About what? asked Tuk.

You wouldn't believe it, said Huk, but Lydia thought the air was hers and hers alone. And Rupert thought the earth belonged to him and him alone. And Milton thought the water belonged solely to him.

But why? asked Tuk, looking confused.

They kept arguing, continued Huk, saying the earth is mine, the air is mine, the water is mine!

All this quarreling started to annoy a friendly toad, named Toad, who lived on the other side of the island. One day, totally fed up, he hopped over and told these three frogs to stop bickering. But they didn't listen to him.

Then there was a heavy rainstorm and it started to flood their little island in the middle of Rainbow Pond. The island got smaller and smaller, and the frogs got scared. They had nowhere to go. But then they spotted a rock and on it, huddled together, they trembled from cold and fright.

They felt better being close together as they clung to each other for dear life.

When the rain stopped and the water receded, they noticed to their utter amazement that the rock was not a rock. It was Toad who had saved them.

That's a really nice tale, said Tuk. It's a good story to make you feel connected to each other.

But there's more, said Huk. Listen! Those quarrelsome frogs now started *sharing* the water, the earth and the air. They jumped into the water together, they leaped after butterflies together and they finally rested in the weeds together. They were happy frogs now. And Toad was happy too, because the island was finally quiet and peaceful.

I never knew there was such an interesting story about Rainbow Pond, said Tuk. First they shared their fears, and then they shared what they originally thought was theirs alone.

That's right, said Huk, I guess they figured out sharing was more fun.

Soon Huk and Tuk fell asleep on the side of Rainbow Pond. The sun had made them sleepy.

When Tuk woke up, he started to think about the story and couldn't figure out why someone, in this case a frog named Lydia, would claim the air was hers. The air was not *only* hers. Don't we all need air? Don't we all need water and earth? And even though you might claim the air is yours, you're also going to need water and earth. That's probably why they quarreled all the time — because they also needed what the others had and claimed was only theirs too.

The question, thought Tuk, is how do I decide that something is *mine*? Do *I* decide that? Are there rules for what is mine and not mine? Can someone take what is mine and then claim it belongs to them?

I can decide my body and my thoughts and feelings are mine. But when I share my thoughts and feelings, they are no longer mine alone.

It seems that these frogs thought if they shared the air, the water and the earth, it wouldn't be theirs anymore. Is that what they were really afraid of? So many questions were swimming in Tuk's head.

When Huk woke up, Tuk looked at him and decided that sharing tails or tales really does make you feel more connected and closer to each other. And it makes you feel more you!

But, Tuk thought, they also trust each other.

Maybe the frogs didn't trust each other at first. Once when they learned they could trust each other when they huddled together in the storm, they too were able to share things — and to share *in* things.

When they started to share *in* the world of air, earth and water, a world so much greater than they were, they weren't afraid of sharing anymore, afraid of losing what they claimed was theirs.

But what if you share your thoughts and feelings with others and some people make fun of you or think your thoughts and feelings don't matter? Isn't it better not to share and just keep to yourself?

Maybe you can't share and "hold tails" with everyone. Huk and Tuk figured that out from a long time ago.

But maybe you can learn to "hold tails" with someone you didn't think you could, just like Lydia, Milton and Rupert did.

Tuk liked this tale about Rainbow Pond and liked sharing tales — and tails — with Huk.

The Earth is not yours,
Becuse erry one should shear
the worbl. shearing makes people
fell good.

by Anmar Alani

How Do We Come to Know What We Don't Know?

— Fish is Fish by Leo Lionni —

Hey, said Tuk, speaking of ponds, do you know about this tale?

Which one? asked Huk.

The one about fish is fish, said Tuk.

Fish is fish? That sounds strange, said Huk. No, I don't know that one. But pour me some tea first, please. Tea goes well with storytelling.

Tuk poured some tea into Huk's cup and began.

In a pond, at the edge of the woods, lived a minnow and a tadpole. They were best friends.

Rainbow Pond? asked Huk.

No, not Rainbow Pond, said Tuk. I forget the name of this pond, but it was at the edge of the woods. Let's call it Fish Pond.

These best friends, Tuk continued, spent a lot of time together swimming among the weeds, chasing

9

each other and having the kind of fun friends have together.

Then one day, the tadpole grew two tiny legs. Hey, he said, I'm a frog.

Nonsense, the minnow said, last night you were a little fish just like me.

You can imagine how they argued and argued, until the tadpole finally concluded, frogs are frogs and fish is fish.

That didn't really settle the argument, did it? asked Huk.

No, not really, said Tuk.

Anyway, one day, this tadpole — a real frog now — decided to climb out of the pond and onto the bank.

The minnow, by the way, was all grown up too and was a full-fledged fish by now.

But the frog did not return, and the fish wondered where his friend had gone.

But with a splash, the frog returned to the pond one day and the fish was overjoyed to see his friend again.

The frog began to talk about everything he had seen — birds and cows and people.

The minnow — now a fish, remember — listened intently, but couldn't quite picture all these creatures the frog was talking about in his mind.

So, the birds have fins? the fish asked.

Oh, no! said the frog.

Do the cows have gills?

No, no! said the frog.

How about the people, do they have scales?

Nooo! cried the frog.

The fish was exhausted from trying to understand what his friend was talking about.

And the frog was exhausted from trying to explain what his friend couldn't seem to understand.

That's pretty sad, said Huk. I guess that explains frogs are frogs and fish is fish.

Yes, said Tuk, but listen...

The fish was so curious that he decided to see for himself what frog was talking about. So, one day, with a whack of his tail, he threw himself onto the bank.

In a matter of seconds, he couldn't breathe and could only cry out a feeble, help!

It was a good thing his friend the frog was nearby. The frog pushed him back into the pond, where the fish could instantly breathe freely again, letting the water run through his gills.

So happy to be alive, the fish agreed: frogs are frogs and fish is fish.

So is the fish ever going to understand what the world of birds and cows and people is like? asked Huk.

That's a good question, said Tuk.

How do we get to understand something we don't know anything about? I mean, the fish is familiar with his watery world, and that's all he knows.

So how can he come to know anything about the frog's world? He doesn't have the context for understanding it. And jumping out of the water sure didn't help!

This got Huk and Tuk thinking. And just as drinking tea is good for storytelling, it is also good for thinking. Huk and Tuk poured the leftover tea into their cups.

So ... you can listen closely — and that's what the fish did — but that didn't help.

You can ask questions, but that didn't help much, either.

You can try to imagine what the other world is like, but that also didn't help.

Then, as out of one mouth, Huk and Tuk cried out: It's *not* like being in the water!

So, Tuk said, maybe if the fish understood that his friend's world was a world completely different from the world he knew, he could now listen in a different way.

What does that mean? asked Huk.

Well, instead of imagining birds having fins and gills and scales, said Tuk, he'd understand that they didn't look anything like that.

He could start listening to his friend without comparing what his friend said to what he knew about his own world.

That way he could also ask better questions, like how *do* they breathe without gills? And if they don't have scales, what does their skin look like? And if they don't have fins, how do they move around?

See, if you don't just focus on the possible commonalities, like people *also* having fins and gills, then maybe you get a better idea of how different different can be.

Oh, said Huk, this is exciting, imagine all these worlds out there we know nothing about and how much we can learn if we stop comparing things to what we know.

by Aira Aurellano

by Lenard Guerrero

Why We Are in Need of Friendship

— *Alexander and the Wind-Up Mouse* by Leo Lionni —

After some time of shared quiet, Huk turned to Tuk and said, even though the minnow and the tadpole seemed the same at first, it turned out that they were actually very different from one another. But there is one tale that tops that one in that regard.

Do you remember the tale about Alexander, the real mouse who lived in a hole in the baseboard, and Willy, the wind-up mouse?

Oh, I do, said Tuk, but tell the tale again, it is one of my favorites. Tell me while we walk to Pebble Path.

While they walked, Huk began, every now and then, Alexander, a plain mouse, would come out of his hole in the baseboard to look for crumbs and such to eat.

But when the people who lived in the house saw him, they chased him with a broom, and threw cups and saucers or anything that they could find at him.

Poor, poor Alexander; nobody loved him. And sometimes he felt sad and lonely in his little hideout.

Yeah, said Tuk, I remember feeling really bad for him. I never understood why they hated him so. He was only a mouse.

Well, one day, when no one was around, Huk continued, Alexander roamed around the house and suddenly heard a squeak. So he went to see what it was.

That's how Alexander met Willy, the wind-up mouse. Willy was Annie's favorite toy.

Who's Annie? asked Tuk.

Annie was the little girl who lived in the house, said Huk. And not just Annie loved Willy. Everybody who lived there did.

Willy was a toy mouse, and instead of having legs, he had two little wheels and a key on his back to wind him up. When he was wound up, he would run around in circles.

Alexander and Willy became best friends — like the minnow and the tadpole — and every chance he got, Alexander would spend with Willy.

But when Alexander was back in his hole in the baseboard, he could not help but think how he too wanted to be loved like Willy. He realized how he envied him.

Tuk interrupted Huk. Let me ask you this, Huk, would you rather be Alexander, the real mouse, or Willy, the wind-up mouse?

Why do you ask? asked Huk.

Well, said Tuk, because nobody loved Alexander, who was a real mouse, but everybody loved Willy, the wind-up mouse. Would you rather be loved or not loved by everybody?

Wait a minute, said Huk, these are two very different questions.

Of course, I would rather be a real mouse. What a silly question.

And of course, I would want to be loved. What a silly question.

And you make it sound as if you cannot be a real mouse and be loved.

You're right, said Tuk. But would you rather be a real mouse or a wind-up mouse?

A real mouse, said Huk, *even if* nobody loved me.

Now let me continue with the story, said Huk.

But let's sit here for a bit so we can look down on the valley. You can see Pebble Path from here. It's not very far.

One day, Huk continued, Willy told Alexander a strange story. He told him about a magic lizard who lived at the end of Pebble Path and who could change one animal into another.

Is that how Pebble Path got its name? Tuk wanted to know.

Perhaps, said Huk, but sometimes it's hard to know how something got its name.

Anyway, Alexander didn't think twice. He wanted to become a wind-up mouse like Willy. He too wanted to be loved by everybody. And he ran off, desperate to see the lizard. The lizard told him to bring him a purple pebble when the moon was round.

Alexander looked for days to find a purple pebble. No luck!

When he finally returned to the house, he spotted a big box with toys ready to be thrown out and suddenly saw that Willy was in the box.

Alexander ran to the box. He was horrified. Willy explained that Annie had had a birthday party, and everyone had come with a gift. And so the old toys were going to be tossed out.

Alexander's heart cringed. He was a real mouse, remember, and he had a real heart.

But then to his utter amazement, Alexander saw a purple pebble. He picked it up and ran back to the lizard. The moon was round, and he called out, lizard, lizard.

In a flash, the lizard appeared and asked Alexander what he wanted to be.

Oh, now I remember why I love this story so much, said Tuk, and his eyes lit up. Alexander suddenly changed his mind and asked the lizard to change Willy into a real mouse like himself.

Yeah, said Huk, that's right. He decided it's better to be a real mouse, even if nobody loves you.

So what's so special about being a real mouse?

Huk and Tuk thought about this for a while.

Well, said Tuk, I'd rather be a real mouse, so I could make my own decisions. Nobody may love me, but nobody is going to toss me out, either.

Huh, said, Huk, and I'd rather be a real mouse, because I could run away and not depend on someone winding me up with a key.

And, said Tuk, I'd rather be a real mouse and be able to eat delicious cheese.

And — they were starting to have fun with this — I'd rather be a real mouse, said Huk, because I could save my friend with the help of the lizard and a purple pebble under a full moon.

Huk and Tuk were amazed at all the reasons they could come up with why it was so much better to be a real mouse than a toy mouse.

To be a real mouse — or a real anything — Huk and Tuk concluded, is to have free will, the free will to make your own decisions pretty much about anything, from eating delicious cheese to running away from danger.

Poor Willy had no free will. He was only a toy mouse, with little wheels instead of legs and a key on his back. Only when someone wound the key could he move about, running around in circles.

You know, said Huk, if you think about it, even plants make decisions, such as where to get the most nutrients out of the soil.

So anyway, Huk continued, Alexander and Willy were friends — best friends — when Alexander was a real mouse and Willy was not a real mouse.

Now, however, they could be best friends forever!

You know, said Tuk, I love this story because it's a great tale about the importance of friendship. I mean *real* friendship.

Real friendship is based on wanting the best for the other. Willy knew Alexander was sad, and he wanted to make him happy. That's why he told him about the lizard, so Alexander could become a wind-up mouse like him and be loved by everybody.

And then Alexander wanted the best for Willy. By changing him into a real mouse, he wouldn't be thrown out with the other toys. He wanted to save Willy and he wanted to save their friendship.

A real friendship is more than the sum of two friends.

And a not-real friendship? asked Huk

A not-real friendship is less than the sum of two friends.

And it's not always easy to tell the difference.

What do you mean? asked Huk.

Willy was Annie's favorite toy and everybody loved him. Yet, one day he was put in the box of toys ready to be thrown away, said Tuk.

Would they have thrown him out if the friendship was really real?

Yeah, that's a good question, said Huk. And you know, Tuk, come to think of it, up to this day I still have my favorite toy, a magic lizard and a purple pebble too!

Huk and Tuk arrived at Pebble Path when it started to get dark.

We should be heading back home, said Tuk. I'll make dinner.

by Christopher Beltran

What Does It Mean to Be Excluded?

— *The Club* by Arnold Lobel —

Huk and Tuk knew that being friends, and being best friends, meant that they both shared in what is called friendship, and that friendship is more than the sum of two friends.

I remember a tale, said Tuk, after they had finished their dinner at Tuk's house, about how our friend Grasshopper was once included and then excluded from a club of beetles celebrating morning.

It all happened without him even being aware of how it all happened. One moment, Grasshopper belonged to the club, and the next thing you know, Grasshopper was thrown out of the club.

That's terrible! How did *that* happen? asked Huk.

Tuk told the story of how Grasshopper was going down the road when he suddenly saw a bunch of signs all saying something about how wonderful morning is.

One said, Morning is Tops, and another said, Three Cheers for Morning.

Grasshopper concluded that there was a celebration of morning going on. He liked that, because he also liked morning.

He then came across a group of beetles all carrying signs.

Being curious by nature, Grasshopper asked what was going on. One of the beetles explained that they were all in the We Love Morning Club.

The beetles asked Grasshopper whether he, too, liked morning.

Of course he loved morning! Who wouldn't when the sunshine is bright, when the earth sparkles with dew and when the air is crisp?

So, although a grasshopper is certainly not a beetle, Grasshopper was suddenly a member of their club, because he too loved morning.

Oh, said Huk, what a wonderful group of beetles to bring Grasshopper into their club like that.

Yeah, said Tuk, they loved his kind face and made him a member because he loved morning just like they did.

But while the beetles were delighted to have a new member in the club, things suddenly went very wrong very quickly for Grasshopper.

Grasshopper just loves life and so he loves not only morning, but afternoon and night too. He loves the whole day!

I love the whole day too, said Huk.

So what went wrong? Huk wanted to know.

It was a morning club, said Tuk.

But he loved the morning, said Huk. I don't get it, Tuk. He loved morning and it was a morning club. So what's wrong with that?

It was a morning *only* club, Tuk explained. You were supposed to love *only* morning and nothing else.

That sounds a lot like the three quarrelsome frogs, said Huk, with their the earth is mine and mine *only*, or the water is mine and mine *only*, or the air is mine and mine *only*.

Yeah, this business about *only* this or that is worrisome, said Tuk. If Grasshopper *didn't* love morning, he couldn't belong to the morning club — that makes sense. But why wasn't he allowed to love the other parts of the day too?

If you love afternoon and night too, does that mean you love morning *less?*

This got Huk and Tuk wondering.

Maybe that's it, said Huk. Maybe the beetles who love *only* morning think that to love afternoon and night too somehow takes away from their love of morning.

Is that true? asked Tuk.

Does love work that way? That would mean that there's only so much love to go around, so if you love something else too, then it takes away from what you loved originally.

No, Huk and Tuk said, and they both shook their heads, that can't be true.

Suddenly Tuk had an idea. You know how I think it works? Tuk said.

It really is like the frogs who were afraid of sharing. They wanted to make sure that what was theirs would stay theirs, and sharing somehow meant giving up what was theirs alone.

But then they figured out that sharing worked the other way around. Now that they were able to share in everything, they had more of everything, not less. They had the air and the earth *and* the water.

So, concluded Huk, I guess the beetles could have learned from Grasshopper that you can love the whole day and it doesn't mean you have to love morning less, but instead, they threw him out of the club.

Yeah, said Tuk. They threw him out and they took back his wreath and the sign they had given him, and they called him names like *stupid* and *dummy*.

But it sounds more like *they* were stupid and dumb, suggested Huk, for not asking Grasshopper why he liked afternoon and night too.

It reminds me of the fish who might have asked the frog if land creatures don't breathe through gills, how do they breathe? said Huk.

It was the morning *only* club, said Tuk, so they weren't even interested in afternoon and night.

Fair enough, said Huk, but that still doesn't mean it's okay to be rude to him and call him names.

Why did they do that?

They were afraid, I think, said Tuk.

And so, when you're afraid, it's okay to be rude?

No, it's not okay, but it happens. In fact, it happens all the time.

Reminds me of the poor wind-up mouse, Willy, who was loved one day and tossed in a box to be thrown out with other toys the next, said Huk.

I don't like those beetles, said Huk. They're just plain mean. If they like Grasshopper enough to make him a member of their club, they could've been nice to him even when he said he loved afternoon and night.

They didn't think of it like that, said Tuk. They didn't feel they had to be nice to anyone who didn't love only morning.

Grasshopper, though, was not going to let the beetles ruin his day.

You know, Grasshopper loves the world, and so he just picked up and kept on walking. He loves the journey more than anything else anyway.

He saw the bright sunshine, he noticed the earth sparkling with dew and he felt the crisp, fresh air as he went on down the road.

Huk and Tuk agreed with Grasshopper. The whole day is beautiful — morning, noon and night.

by Ximena Jimenez

by Matthew Cardenas

We love morning club

popcorn

sofa

water

by Laisha Delgado

What Does It Mean to Be Included?

— *The Voyage* by Arnold Lobel —

Grasshopper didn't mind that he no longer belonged to the morning only club anymore, but he didn't like the way the beetles had treated him.

He didn't like the way they excluded him from the club, calling him *stupid* and *dummy* and snatching his wreath and sign away like that.

Oh, said Huk, that reminds me of another story about Grasshopper.

The evening is young, said Tuk, so tell me this one too, before we turn in for the night.

This time, Huk said, Grasshopper came across a mosquito called Mosquito.

Oh, I think I know who you mean, said Tuk, Mosquito who takes riders in his little boat from one side of the puddle to the other?

Yes, but to Mosquito that puddle is a lake, said Huk.

Then we should call it Puddle Lake, suggested Tuk.

Mosquito had been carrying riders across Puddle Lake, Huk began, for as long as he could remember.

To get his riders across Puddle Lake safely, he had strict rules.

When Grasshopper got to Puddle Lake, which really just looked like a small puddle in the road to him, he met Mosquito.

Rules are rules, Mosquito told Grasshopper. You have to get into my boat if you want to safely get to the other side.

Grasshopper was a bit confused. He didn't want to offend Mosquito, but he knew he was way, way too big to get into the boat. Didn't Mosquito realize that?

He didn't, because he kept telling Grasshopper that rules are rules.

Grasshopper had looked and decided he could easily jump to the other side, but the beetles had been rude to Grasshopper and he wasn't going to be rude to Mosquito.

And besides, Grasshopper is not a rude kind of grasshopper.

So, what happened? asked Tuk.

Tuk was really curious how Grasshopper was going to solve this problem, because there was no way he could ever get into Mosquito's tiny boat, even if rules are rules.

Well, he could have just walked — or rather hopped — away, said Huk.

He could have ignored Mosquito and his rules altogether.

But he didn't do that.

Then, what *did* he do? asked Tuk.

What would you have done? asked Huk.

Tuk shook his head. He really didn't know what to say.

Well, Grasshopper came up with a very wise idea, Huk told Tuk.

He picked up Mosquito's ferry and walked across Puddle Lake with it.

When Mosquito felt the boat moving, he called out, All aboard!

Mosquito got excited and told Grasshopper all about taking riders across for many years and how he was never afraid of storms and waves.

Grasshopper listened to Mosquito.

When they got to the other side, Grasshopper put Mosquito's boat down.

Mosquito was proud to have safely carried Grasshopper across Puddle Lake and told him he now had to get back to get new riders.

Grasshopper thanked Mosquito for safely taking him across the lake.

Huh? said Tuk. How did Mosquito not realize that it was Grasshopper who had carried the boat across the lake?

His world only includes very small insects that can fit in his boat, said Huk, and his rules are to carry those creatures safely across Puddle Lake.

He can't see that his rules don't apply to Grasshopper. In his mind, Grasshopper should also get into the boat — if he wants to get to the other side, that is.

But rules don't always apply, said Tuk.

No, of course not, said Huk. They only apply in certain cases — cases the rules are made for.

But Mosquito thought they applied to *everything* and *everyone*, said Tuk. It reminds me of the fish who thought the way of the watery world applied to everybody too, and so birds and cows and people must all have fins, and scales and gills too.

Yeah, folks get carried away, said Huk, and forget what rules are for. They just remember, rules are rules, like Mosquito did.

Grasshopper decided to respect Mosquito and Mosquito's rules, even when they didn't apply to him. So he picked up the boat instead of hopping across Puddle Lake.

And Grasshopper even thanked Mosquito for taking him safely across the lake.

He thanked Mosquito? asked Tuk.

Yes, said Huk, perhaps simply to be kind to Mosquito and to include him in the journey across Puddle Lake.

Hmm, said Huk, I like that idea of being kind and including him, just because.

by Marc Guaro

by Amaris Rodriguez

Why We Are in Need of Keeping Our Eyes Open

— *Cookies* by Arnold Lobel —

The next morning, Huk and Tuk set out for the hills nearby.

I have a question, said Tuk. How do we figure out when rules apply and when they don't? I mean, obviously Mosquito's rules didn't apply to Grasshopper because he was way too big for Mosquito's ferry.

But I'm sure there are times it is not so obvious.

Like when? asked Huk.

Let's say there is a rule to not eat animals, said Tuk. But what if you are in a situation where the only way to *survive* is to eat an animal?

Do the rules apply only to everyday life, or to situations of life and death, too?

Well, said Huk, I'd rather die than eat an animal.

And I, said Tuk, would most certainly kill and eat an animal in order to survive.

Hmm..., thought Huk.

How does one decide if a rule applies to you or not? And would Tuk get in trouble for not following the rule because Tuk desperately wanted to stay alive?

Is there a rule about rules? Huk asked.

Good question, said Tuk. Are we responsible for deciding whether to follow a rule or not? And does it mean we are not personally responsible if we blindly follow the rule? I mean, if I follow the rule, is the rule ultimately responsible for how I act?

Oh my, said Huk, this is complicated. I guess, if it's my decision to follow the rule, it is ultimately my responsibility, too. I mean, I can't hide behind the rule and blame the rule if things don't work out right. I can only blame myself for following a rule I should not have followed.

So is the rule about rules, that whatever the rule, I am ultimately responsible for following it or not? asked Huk.

That sounds about right, concluded Tuk.

Hey, said Tuk, do you remember our buddies Frog and Toad, who live near Pebble Path close to where the magic lizard lives?

Yes, of course I remember Frog and Toad, said Huk. What about them?

Well, Tuk continued, there's a funny story going around about how Frog and Toad were trying to figure out what rules to use to stop eating Toad's delicious fresh-baked cookies so they wouldn't get sick.

Tell me, said Huk.

One day, said Tuk, Toad decided to bake some cookies and bring them over to Frog's house so they could enjoy them together.

Toad had made a lot of cookies. They were so good that they couldn't stop eating them.

At some point, Frog pointed out that if they didn't stop, they'd start feeling sick.

While they both agreed they should really stop, they couldn't help eating one more last cookie and then one more very last cookie after that.

So, this rule was obviously not working. Something else was needed.

Toad had agreed with Frog that they needed to stop eating the cookies, but how do you stop doing something you really want to do?

Frog explained that you need willpower. Because willpower is the rule that makes you stop doing what you don't want to stop doing.

Toad had been quiet for a bit and then said, like not eating any more very last cookies?

That's right, Frog said, put the cookies in a box and then I'll put them high up on the shelf. That'll work. Then we can follow our rule.

But we can break the rule by taking the box down and opening the box, Toad suggested.

Well, said Frog, then we'll tie a string around the box. Then we can follow the rule.

What good is a rule if you can take the box down from the shelf, cut the string and open the box? You can see where this was going, said Tuk. Nowhere!

So, I guess, said Huk, they couldn't follow their own rules?

Does that mean they didn't have any willpower?

I'm not so sure, said Tuk, because they seemed to be trying. They were thinking of ways to make themselves stick to the rule of eating no more cookies.

But then Frog had a bright idea, Tuk continued. He took the box outside and emptied it, calling out, Hey birds, here are cookies!

And guess what? Gone were the cookies. Just like that.

Okay, said Huk, there are no more cookies to eat. Does that mean they followed their own rule? I'm not so sure.

Throwing the cookies to the birds took the problem away and so the need for willpower didn't come into play anymore either.

But didn't it take willpower to throw the cookies out? asked Tuk.

I think it's more like following a rule with your eyes closed, said Huk, because they didn't have to make any effort to not eat the cookies anymore. With the cookies gone, the rule to not eat any more cookies was also gone. And the willpower was gone too. Gone!

So, is it self-deception to follow rules with your eyes closed? asked Tuk.

Self-deception? asked Huk. Explain.

You think you're following the rules and you make-believe you're following the rules, said Tuk, but you're not following anything, because there's nothing to follow. Tuk was sounding very philosophical.

How come there's nothing to follow? asked Huk.

Because, said Tuk, if you get rid of the problem, there is nothing to follow.

It's like that ancient tale about Oedipus. Remember? The oracle of Delphi told Oedipus that he was going to kill his father and marry his mother.

So to get rid of the problem — kind of like what Frog did by throwing the cookies to the birds — he left his home in the city of Corinth and fled to a faraway place called Thebes. That way he could not kill his father and marry his mother, who both lived in Corinth.

But Thebes is exactly where he ended up killing his *real* father and marrying his *real* mother, who both lived in Thebes.

Having been warned by an oracle that their son would slay his father, Oedipus's mother had abandoned Oedipus when he was born. A shepherd had found him and brought him to Corinth, where the king and queen of Corinth adopted him.

So that's how Oedipus left Corinth and ended up in Thebes.

Getting rid of a problem is not solving it, Huk and Tuk agreed.

So, said Huk, Frog and Toad should have found a way to keep the cookies *and* not eat them.

Does that mean that willpower only makes sense when your eyes are wide open? asked Tuk.

Yes, said Huk, your eyes wide open and the bowl of cookies right in front of them.

If you blindly follow the rules, you don't have to be or feel responsible for anything.

You make yourself *believe* you are being responsible, because you are doing your duty by following the rules, but in fact you are not taking any responsibility at all. You're just blindly following the rules. That's a cop-out really, and that's called self-deception.

Oh, thought Tuk, who was getting to understand how self-deception works.

So Huk and Tuk decided that if you don't want to deceive yourself, you should keep your eyes wide open.

They knew that when you walk through the woods or up on the hills, you have to keep your eyes wide open. And it really seems to be a good rule overall. There are always twists and turns in life no matter where you go.

Sometimes it seems so much easier to just go along with some rule and not think too much about it, Huk decided. And when someone questions you, you just say, well, I followed the rule the way I was supposed to.

Figuring things out for yourself is a whole different can of worms — I mean bowl of cookies, Huk added with a smile.

Huk and Tuk liked this tale and — taking full responsibility now — figured they should go home and bake some delicious cookies.

I am going to
baske ackase

by Alexa Garcia

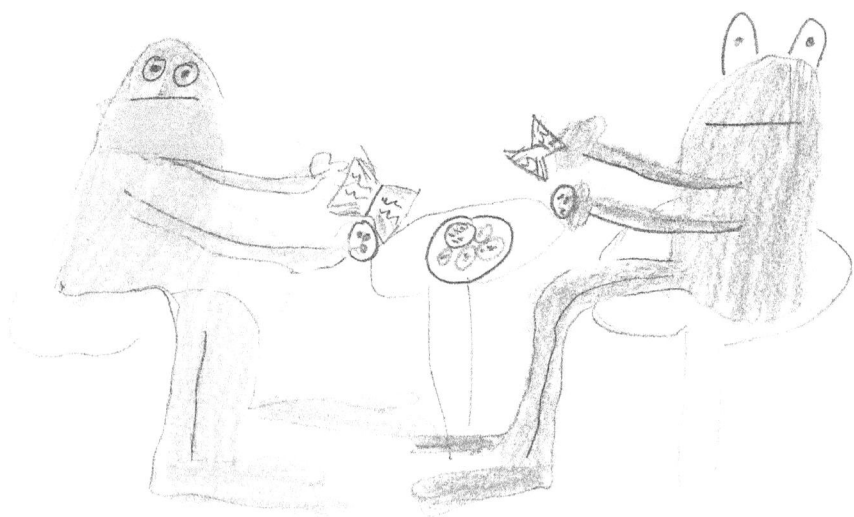

by Adriana Perez

by Johnny Tejeda Rodriquez

by Laisha Delgado

References

Fingarette, Herbert. *Self-Deception*. New York: Humanities Press, 1969.

Lionni, Leo. *Alexander and the Wind-Up Mouse*. New York: Dragonfly Books, 1969.

———. *Fish is Fish*. New York: Dragonfly Books, 1970.

———. *It's Mine*. New York: Dragonfly Books, 1985.

Lobel, Arnold. "The Club," in *Grasshopper on the Road*. New York: Harper & Row, Publishers, 1978.

———. "Cookies," in *Frog and Toad Together*. New York: Harper & Row, Publishers, 1972.

———. "The Voyage," in *Grasshopper on the Road*. New York: Harper & Row, Publishers, 1978.

Acknowledgements

First and foremost, I would like to acknowledge the teachers and students at El Toyon Elementary School in National City, California. For the past three years, I have conducted classes in philosophy with children from first to third grade. After I read them a picture book story, the children philosophize about some of the questions that come up for them in the story. Was it fair for the beetles to throw Grasshopper out of the We Love Morning Club? Do Frog and Toad really have willpower? How can you tell something is yours and only yours? After our group discussions, the children write their thoughts about the story and draw pictures.

The wonderful teachers I've worked with — Yen Dang, Silvia Toledo, Patricia Carrillo, Pat Duran and Elizabeth McEvoy — have really appreciated how doing philosophy with children has gotten the children to think for themselves. Yen Dang supported the Philosophy with Children program from its inception and promoted the program among her colleagues. Yen Dang's and Patricia Carrillo's students provided the drawings for this little book.

I am thankful for the invaluable feedback my friend and colleague Claartje van Sijl provided throughout my writing process. I always felt free to bounce my ideas off her, and I have enjoyed our monthly Skype calls.

And, of course, I am very grateful always to Mr. Lizzard to whom I dedicated my first little book.

I also want to thank the Iguana Books team who feel like family by now, and especially Holly Warren, who edited both *Why We Are in Need of Tails* and *Why We Are in Need of Tales*. As an editor, she is truly inspiring.

Maria daVenza Tillmanns

Maria teaches a "Philosophy with Children" program in underserved San Diego schools in partnership with the University of California, San Diego. In 1980, she attended Dr. Matthew Lipman's workshop on philosophy for children and later wrote her dissertation on philosophical counseling and teaching under the direction of Martin Buber scholar Dr. Maurice Friedman. She has publications in a number of international journals. For Maria, philosophy is an art form, and she enjoys painting with ideas. Philosophy has helped her navigate the world in all its complexity, including having a multicultural background and having been raised in the US as well as in the Netherlands. She came back to the US to study and moved across the Atlantic multiple times.

www.ingramcontent.com/pod-product-compliance
Lightning Source LLC
Chambersburg PA
CBHW031633040426
42452CB00007B/806